Bulletin Board Ideas

For Weekday and Sunday School Teachers

Bulletin Board Ideas

For *Weekday* and Sunday School Teachers

James H. and
Rowena D. Robinson

CONCORDIA
Publishing House
St. Louis

Contents

Concordia Publishing House St. Louis, Missouri

Copyright © 1973 Concordia Publishing House
Library of Congress Catalog Card No. 72-94108
ISBN 0-570-03141-9

MANUFACTURED IN THE UNITED STATES OF AMERICA

PART I
Construction Helps and Hints

Bulletin boards are a very important part of a child's educational environment. This is especially true of the short time he is studying about his Lord and Savior in the church school. An effective teacher will want to use every available means to teach God's children the great teachings of His Word.

Although children are accustomed to having bulletin boards present common school subjects, we do have some special considerations to remember in using boards for Christian education. Children may see them only once or twice a week and for only one to two hours at a time. Therefore its message must be clear and to the point. They must also be attractive, interesting, and current. These requirements present an interesting challenge to the church school teacher.

It is the purpose of this booklet to give guidelines and suggestions to you, the teacher, in using the bulletin board as a teaching tool. It is designed to help you motivate your children to worship and serve God, to introduce topics of study, and to teach concepts. May it help you to better equip the lambs of Christ for Christian living and service.

The themes can be used as designed. But more often you will want to make adjustments to your own situation according to materials, time, and space available.

As you become a collector of items suitable for use on bulletin boards, you will want to be creative in designing your own. Be sure to record your ideas for future use.

Many teachers collect pictures and other items for bulletin boards over a period of many years. Usually you can use a board design two or three times without changing mounts or letters. File items in a large manila envelope and place in a file under the main seasons of the church year. When you wish to use the design, you need only change an item or so and you are ready to assemble your design. If you so choose, you may use a different background to vary the total effect. Another helpful idea is to have two or three basic designs for each season which you can alternate over several years.

Yet another idea which is great for busy teachers, especially vacation Bible school teachers, is to have ladies or youth gather pictures from old magazines and give them general mounts. Cut out letters and make whatever cutouts are necessary and make into a kit. This way pictures can be swapped until you have good illustrations of the theme or lesson you wish to teach.

Now let's explore some possibilities for designs in the basic areas to consider in planning bulletin boards: the background, lettering, pictures, cutouts, and small objects.

Backgrounds and borders: Choosing the correct material and color for the background is very important, for it is the background which often sets the mood of a board.

There are many different materials available for the background. Some are more practical than others. For church schools the most practical backgrounds are large (24"×36") sheets or rolls of construction paper. These come in many colors and can be obtained from most school supply companies. These are also easy to staple to the boards.

Large sheets of corrugated paper are also useful. Though more expensive, they can be rolled up and stored for use at a later time. These also can be purchased in many colors at school supplies.

Shelf paper, gift wrapping, foil or tissue paper may be purchased at many stores. Most of the large rolls of shelf paper come in pastel shades and are good with dark letters and border.

Different types of wallpaper can be used for special backgrounds. Tweeds, paneling, brick, or rock add interest in texture. Try not to use bright floral designs, plaids, or stripes which lead to confusion or distract from the design itself or the message.

Burlap comes in many lovely colors and can provide a different texture or contrast to work with. This is a great background for designs that are arrangements of pictures and letters only. When the design is simple, made up only of pictures and letters, burlap background will enhance your display. Another way to make a simple board more attractive is to add construction paper in an unusual free form to the background. Or outline a free form with yarn on the burlap. These free-form shapes may hold one or several pictures or cutouts.

You may wish to try other materials for backgrounds. Any material or paper with enough body to it may be used, such as felt, corduroy, plastics, or cork.

On some occasions you may want to complete the background by adding a border. This is especially true if your board is not framed. Here we must also think of texture. If your background is corrugated paper, a border of construction paper is good. If on the other hand your background is construction paper, you can achieve interest and texture by choosing corrugated paper for the border. You may use several different types of borders on burlap backgrounds. You can also use the same type of paper for both background and border if you show contrast in color. You will also want to keep texture in mind when choosing the material for the letters and cutouts you plan to use. You may also find an interesting effect by using wallpaper paneling for a border if you do not have your board framed. Be sure to miter the corners when using this material.

Lettering: The caption of the bulletin board carries the written message or theme of the design. Because of its importance, it deserves special attention. It should be to the point and not too long. The caption may also be in the form of a question. Many Bible verses make great captions. Above all, the caption must be legible.

The caption can be of individual letters. For the primary-age child who is just learning to read, basic manuscript-type capital and lowercase letters should be used. For the middle and upper grades you may use all capitals or all lowercase letters, or interesting arrangements and combinations of different sizes of one style. With different types of design you may want to use other styles of lettering. Cursive lettering may also be used. This can be achieved with yarns, or you can purchase letters of construction paper to cut out.

For the busy teacher, letter patterns are a must. These may be obtained in several sizes from local school supply companies or stationery stores. A basic 3″ capital letter and its companion lowercase letter is best for the 3′×4′ board; 2″ and 4″ letters are also good. Patterns also come in larger and smaller sizes.

These cutout letters can be made of several types of materials. A variety of paper makes the best letters. These could be construction, corrugated, wallpaper, metallic, velour, gift wrapping, poster board, manila, oak tag, commercial package boxes from cereal or mixes, newspapers, magazines; other materials such as cloth, art pellon, twigs, and sticks, Reynolds Wrap and other foil, yarn, vinyls, felt, straws, or pipe cleaners. You may also combine two colors or textures for double-mount letters for an interesting effect.

There are also letters available at school supplies which are ready to punch or cut out as you need them. They come in several colors and sizes. Some are made of construction paper; others are of more durable material and can be used over and over again. These are very handy and inexpensive.

A more expensive but very convenient letter is the pin-back plastic display letter. These three-dimensional letters come in capitals and lowercase with punctuation marks and numerals. They are available in several sizes in white, red, and black. These letters, which come in storage trays and can be used for years, have many uses and are especially good for the small classroom.

Captions may also be printed, drawn, or written on paper or other material such as art pellon with a felt pen or with liquid embroidery pens which come in many colors. They may also be painted on with brushes or spray-painted using stencils. You may print the caption free hand, or you may use letter guides which come in several sizes. You may also print the captions on different shapes for interesting effects. Use dark lettering and be sure to make the letters large enough, at least one-eighth inch wide. Or use white, yellow, or other light color on black art pellon for interest.

Although it takes less time to put the drawn or printed captions on the board, more space is usually required, and they are often more difficult to arrange. Allow for this in your plan or design. When you use individual letters, the caption can be separated to add interest and emphasis to the message of the board. Individual letters may also be staggered, spaced differently, or by using straight pins and pulling the letters out to the heads of the pins, you can achieve a 3-D effect.

Pictures: Pictures are one of the most effective tools in illustrating bulletin board themes. Be a collector; you can get them from several sources.

a. *Ideals* magazines are an excellent source, giving you 20 to 30 pictures in each issue. There is no advertising, and most pictures are in beautiful color. These are a good source for pictures of seasonal activities and scenic pictures, and the Christmas, Easter, and special issues usually include religious pictures. This company also publishes greeting booklets with colored pictures.

b. News magazines such as *Life, Look, Time,* and *Newsweek* are excellent sources on current events. These may be used in the classroom as teaching pictures or for bulletin board displays.

c. Ladies' magazines are good for family activities.

d. *Colorado* magazine is excellent for Rocky Mountain scenery and recreational activities.

e. *National Geographic* has excellent pictures for background information on countries where we do mission work. They occasionally have helpful articles on the Holy Land.

f. Travel magazines are also worth checking for scenic, vacation, or local activities.

g. Certain sports and teen magazines will give you pictures for activities of the high school and college ages.

h. Church magazines such as *Interaction* and old *This Day* magazines will supply pictures of church activities.

i. Calendars also are excellent sources for pictures. Most religious calendars are good. Major calendar companies will be glad to give their samples or display kits to churches if you can pick them up.

j. Daily or weekly newspapers also provide pictures suitable for bulletin boards. The magazine supplements of Sunday papers often have good colored pictures.

k. Our own church publications, such as the *Reporter,* the *Lutheran Layman,* and *Lutheran Woman's Quarterly* include religious pictures. Though they may be small and in black and white, you can mount several on one page. Many cities also have a monthly Lutheran newspaper.

l. Pictures may also be purchased from local and state organizations and companies. Publishing houses, including our own Concordia, have kits or packets of pictures for missions or Bible stories for sale.

m. Your own District office will have some pictures available on local or District mission work.

n. Check your city or state chamber of commerce for pictures of local activities.

o. Sunday bulletins provide interesting pictures that can be used with many designs. Check with your local religious bookstore for their display books when they are finished with them. Your pastor or church office receives examination packets of bulletins which you may ask for when they have made their selections.

p. Sunday School booklets and pamphlets are an excellent source for Bible stories and related activities.

q. Old textbooks and atlases are good for maps and pictures. Be sure they are up to date with their information.

Correct mounts for the pictures make a plain bulletin board beautiful and attractive. The easiest mounting material for church school teachers is a good grade of construction paper in assorted colors. There will be times when you will want special mounts to make your board more unusual. Excellent frames can be made out of corrugated paper. You may also use a wallpaper paneling for a wooden frame effect. Be sure to miter the corners or use a type of frame which looks more rugged.

When you are displaying several pictures in a seasonal display, use the same color for mounts, such as yellow or orange for fall or Thanksgiving. You may use different shades of one color and still have basic unity.

In most cases one mount is sufficient. It can be a contrast to the picture, or a color that accents part of the picture. You may also want to add a narrow submount to get this effect.

Usually, dark mounts are best if the picture is bright or light. If a picture is somewhat dull, give it life with a proper mount. Before mounting, try several colors to find the best combination.

Rubber cement is good for making the mount permanent. However, with a little effort you can get the picture loose when a new mount is needed. Elmer's glue will work if you don't have rubber cement.

Cutouts and silhouettes: Some themes can be illustrated best with cutouts and silhouettes. These may be purchased at a stationery, gift shop, or school supply company. They may also be made by you or your students as a class or presession activity.

Hallmark home and school decorations can be used for the seasonal designs. They also have animals and patriotic decorations. School supplies carry the Dennison, Eureka, and Trend Enterprise prints and decorative cutouts for many topics including foreign children and flags of other countries. Dennison also has holiday tissue prints for 3-D effect.

Cutouts and silhouettes can be made very easily of many materials. Construction, corrugated, velour, and metallic papers are the most common and practical. But they can also be made from felt, white and black art pellon, plastics, cotton, and other materials.

Many helps and hints are available to assist the busy teacher. You can get patterns and ideas from many sources. There are several good pattern books which can be purchased. Religious coloring books are very useful. Craft books and papercraft books have good ideas for activities which can be used on bulletin boards. And packets of stencils provide patterns suitable for cutouts and silhouettes and symbols. Check your local religious bookstores for all of these helps, or order from your publishing house. A list is compiled for your convenience.

Liquid embroidery companies such as Artex, Tri-Chem, and Cameo offer many patterns that can be used on seasonal and holiday boards. If you make cutouts on art pellon, they will be good for several years. Artex also has religious patterns, such as an open Bible, praying hands, Moses and the tables of stone, pictures of the life of Christ, which can be painted. These companies also have sports figures for boards on teen or adult activities.

At times you may find a pattern that is good but not the size you need. You can enlarge it by marking it off in half-inch squares. Then mark off another sheet in inch squares. Study the design and then draw it into the corresponding larger squares. Practice makes a good design.

You may also get a good cutout by using a pantograph. This little machine can be purchased at school supplies or graphic arts stores for as little as $5.00. With it you can enlarge a pattern many times its size or make it smaller, and it is much more accurate. Follow the directions carefully, and it will be a handy tool for years for all the teachers of your church.

Objects: Many small objects found around the home will add interest to your board. These three-dimensional items may be such things as ribbons, cotton and other material, Easter grass, straws, pipe cleaners, yarn, plastic or real flowers, paper dolls, greeting cards, leaves, or flags.

They may also be larger items such as individual cereal boxes, small children's cake mix boxes or cartons, plastic toy animals and fences such as are found in farm sets, plastic toy tools or dishes, small brushes, perfume or cosmetic boxes, small books or Bibles, small musical instruments, doll clothes, socks, hankies, or combs.

These objects can be difficult to attach to the board. For example, you may want to add rulers, pencil, or such school items to the board. You can make quarter-inch or half-inch brackets of construction paper the color of the object, place the object in these brackets, and staple them to the board. If you are using small boxes, you may need to cut one end out and then staple or pin them to the board.

Another way to display objects is to make little "shelves" of oak tag or heavy poster board on which to place your items. Check craft books for ideas and helps on this.

Although these objects require more work, they are well worth it. A word of caution though: do not let these objects distract from the message you wish to convey to the children. So keep in mind such things as location and color when planning your design.

PART II
Bulletin Boards for the Church Year

A. Advent—Christmas

1. **Advent:** "Come, Lord Jesus"

2. **Source:** Advent of the church year

3. **Special emphasis:** Proper attitudes and preparation for the Christmas season

4. **Aim or purpose:** To use the Advent wreath with its symbolism and pictures of various worship settings to develop an understanding of the real meaning of Christmas

5. **Materials needed**
   a. Light green shelf paper for background
   b. Bright green construction paper for wreath
   c. Ribbon bow
   d. Construction paper for rolled candles
   e. Black construction paper for letters
   f. Pictures showing children in various worship settings

* **Variations**
   a. Place a large picture of the Nativity in the center of the wreath
   b. Use pictures of the Christmas story instead of worship pictures
   c. Make the Advent wreath out of corrugated paper
   d. Shape the candles out of corrugated paper, putting a base and a flame on each; they will hold their shape for several weeks
   e. If you wish, pull the wreath out to the heads of pins for depth
   f. Use a styrofoam ring and add a wreath of green construction paper with red berries. It will be easier to attach the wreath to the board if you buy a ring that is one half or three fourths of an inch thick.

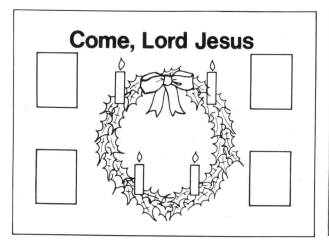

Sacred design

1. **Advent:** "The Lord Is My Light"

2. **Source:** Advent pericopes: Luke 21:25-36 and John 12:44-50

3. **Special emphasis:** The second coming of Christ, when "He shall come to judge the quick and the dead" (Second Article)

4. **Aim or purpose:** To teach the concept that in Advent we also look to Christ's second coming on the Last Day, when we shall understand those things about God which sin has kept secret from us. Then the Lord will bring to light the things now hidden in darkness. (1 Cor. 4:5)

5. **Materials needed**
   a. Lavender construction paper or burlap for the background
   b. Pattern and purple construction paper for six-pointed Creator's star, about 9" or 10"
   c. White paper for letters "The LORD" and for center of flame
   d. Yellow paper for letters "IS MY LIGHT" and for flame
   e. Gold construction paper for candles
   f. Purple construction or corrugated paper for border, 2" to 4" wide depending on size of board

* **Variations**
   a. If your board is large and rectangular, you may add a picture of the Nativity and a picture of Jesus' second coming
   b. You may also use 1' letters and 1 Cor. 4:5 for the caption, especially for older children and adults.

How Series

1. **Advent and Christmas:** "The King of Kings"

2. **Source:** "Lift Up Your Heads, Ye Mighty Gates," *The Lutheran Hymnal,* No. 73; "The Baby King"; Psalm 24

3. **Special emphasis:** Jesus, ruler of the kingdom of God, comes to live in our hearts

4. **Aim or purpose:** To remember that Jesus was the King of kings and to prepare our hearts for His coming; to use pictures to follow the story of the birth of Jesus

5. **Materials needed**
   a. Very light green or white background
   b. Bright green construction paper for tree silhouette
   c. Gold metallic paper for crown
   d. Yellow construction paper for star and straw
   e. Brown paper for manger

   f. Black paper for Chi-Rho and letters

   g. Pictures of the Christmas story on green mounts

* **Variations**

   a. Green corrugated paper works nicely for the tree

   b. If you have straw, you may add it for realism

   c. Use a caption such as ''Are you ready for the King of kings?''

   d. If your board is square, omit the pictures

1. **Christmas:** ''Listen to the Angels Sing''

2. **Source:** ''Hark, the Herald Angels Sing,'' *The Lutheran Hymnal,* No. 94;
   Luke 2:13-14

3. **Special emphasis:** The angels were the first to announce the birth of
   Jesus the Savior

4. **Aim or purpose:** To emphasize the message of the angels to the shepherds as recorded in Luke 2:8-14

5. **Materials needed**

   a. Royal blue construction paper for the background

   b. Net material, such as bridal veiling, for the cloud, use several thicknesses

   c. Metallic paper for notes and stars and ''Glory to God''

   d. Bright yellow construction paper for caption

   e. Yellow border such as Bordette in corrugated paper

   f. White paper for angels and crayons or white pellon and liquid embroidery

   g. Patterns for singing angel cutouts, stars, and notes

   h. Elmer's glue or rubber cement to glue stars, notes, and ''Glory to God'' on the background

---

1. **Christmas:** ''Christmas Peace''

2. **Source:** Advent and Christmas of the church year; Luke 2

3. **Special emphasis:** The major events of the Christmas story, the Nativity, the angel message to the shepherds, the shepherds' adoration of the Baby Jesus

4. **Aim or purpose:** To relate the Christmas story through the use of pictures

5. **Materials needed**
    a. White or light green for the background
    b. Red yarn or construction paper for letters
    c. Green and red construction paper for holly leaves and berries
    d. Red metallic paper for bells
    e. Green corrugated or construction paper for church window mounts of pictures
    f. Patterns for mounts and cutouts
    g. Pictures of the Christmas story such as *Ideals* magazines have

* **Variations**
    a. Choose color combinations found in the pictures you plan to use
    b. Children can make the cutouts; provide them with patterns to save time
    c. Try making the cutouts from corrugated paper; choose bright colors or subdued blues and silvers for a more peaceful effect
    d. If you wish, pull pictures out to the heads of pins to give them accent

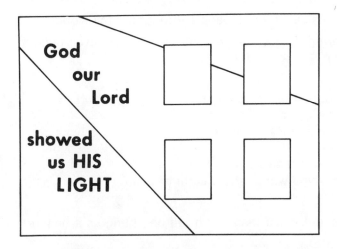

1. **Christmas:** "God Our Lord Showed Us His Light"

2. **Source:** Christmas of the church year; John 1:1-9; 12:44-50

3. **Special emphasis:** Jesus is our light and way to heaven

4. **Aim or purpose:** To learn that Jesus, God's Son, is the true light to everlasting life for every man

5. **Materials needed**
    a. Light blue or aqua for the background
    b. Yellow to show the divine light of God
    c. Bright red for the letters
    d. Pictures of the birth of Christ

* **Variations**
    a. Use any cheerful Christmas colors, such as different shades of green
    b. Use a caption such as "Light of the World" or "The Lord Is My Light"
    c. Begin with a picture of the Annunciation and follow the Christmas story to the coming of the Wise Men; good for the entire Advent and Christmas season

1. **Christmas:** "Joy to the World"

2. **Source:** Christmas and Epiphany of the church year; *The Lutheran Hymnal,* No. 87; John 3:16

3. **Special emphasis:** Jesus came for all people throughout the world

4. **Aim or purpose:** To bring the joyous message that God so loved people that He sent His own Son to be born in a manger

5. **Materials needed**

   a. Light blue or aqua burlap for the background
   b. Royal blue felt for the world
   c. Bright red or red-orange for the letters
   d. Black for the manger
   e. Yellow for the star and streamers
   f. Cutouts of children of the world, about eight of them

* **Variations**

   a. This design is beautiful when made with felt and hung as a banner; use Elmer's glue
   b. It can be used as a poster too, using corrugated, construction, or metallic papers for good texture contrast

---

1. **Christmas:** "Oh, I Love This Jesus"

2. **Source:** Stanza 4 of "In a Little Stable," a primary Christmas hymn

3. **Special emphasis:** Declaring our love for Jesus

4. **Aim or purpose:** To motivate children to learn the song; to illustrate the scene of Jesus' birth with the traditional stable

5. **Materials needed**

   a. A light beige, tan, or natural shelf or construction paper for background
   b. Light blue or aqua construction paper for the church window and letters
   c. Dark brown for the stable
   d. Yellow and orange construction paper for the star

Variations
   a. Try a foil paper for one part of the background
   b. Metallic paper for the star will also add interest
   c. You could also make the stable of scraps of paneling, or use wallpaper paneling and glue it to a piece of cardboard

B. Epiphany—New Year—Missions

Sacred design

1. **Epiphany:** "They Came with Gifts"
2. **Source:** Epiphany of the church year; the Gradual for Epiphany; Matt. 2: 1-12
3. **Special emphasis:** The Wise Men brought gifts when they came to worship the King born in Bethlehem
4. **Aim or purpose:** To teach the Epiphany story of the coming of the Wise Men as found in Matt. 2:1-12
5. **Materials needed**
   a. Large sheets of construction paper in three colors, such as purple, rose, and pink; yellow, yellow-orange, and orange; or any three analogous colors
   b. Black construction paper for kings' heads, gifts, letters, and strips
   c. Patterns for kings, gifts, and 2″ letters

1. **Epiphany:** "God's Star Went Before Them"
2. **Source:** Epiphany of the church year; Is. 60:1
3. **Special emphasis:** The worship of the Wise Men

4. **Aim or purpose:** To establish the concept that God used a special star to lead the Wise Men to search for God's Son, to worship Him and bring gifts. We should also worship Him and bring Him gifts

5. **Materials needed**
   a. White background
   b. Orange for letters
   c. Yellow for Creator's star
   d. Black for star mount and Wise Men
   e. Patterns for letters and Wise Men

* **Variations**
   a. Use large silhouettes of the kings' heads, about 6″ to 8″
   b. Try yellow and orange variegated tissue wrapping paper for the background
   c. Then use black or white letters and cutouts
   d. A black border would finish the design

1. **Epiphany:** "Teachings of God"

2. **Source:** The six chief parts of the Catechism; the Third Commandment, "gladly hear and learn God's Word"

3. **Special emphasis:** Youth and adult education in the Scriptures

4. **Aim or purpose:** To remind teens and adults to attend Bible class

5. **Materials needed**
   a. Divide board into eight sections with different colors of art tissue or construction paper; use yellow for the boxes with the captions
   b. Make symbols of black or white
   c. Use 1″ strips of black construction paper as leading for a stained-glass-window effect
   d. Black letters 2″ high, with red letters for the word "YOU"

* **Variations**
   a. Yellow background
   b. Black letters for "Teachings of God" and "YOU"
   c. Red letters for "How well do" and "know them?"
   d. Symbol silhouettes of black and white

1. **Epiphany:** "Don't Leave God out of Your Education"

2. **Source:** The Child Jesus in the temple, Luke 2:41-52; the Third Commandment, "gladly hear and learn God's Word"

3. **Special emphasis:** Attending weekday school

4. **Aim or purpose**

   a. To remind children to attend weekday school, where they can hear and learn God's Word

   b. Before weekday school begins in the fall, while home visits are being made. To accompany a table display of materials to be used in the classes

5. **Materials needed**

   a. Black construction paper for the background

   b. Orange construction paper for important words in caption

   c. Bright green construction paper for other words

   d. Cutouts of school objects

   e. Large (10" to 12") open Bible, printed on it a verse such as "God is Love" or "He died for all"

How Series

1. **New Year:** "God Bless You with a Happy New Year"

2. **Source:** New Year of the calendar year

3. **Special emphasis:** To wish the viewers God's blessings in the New Year

4. **Aim or purpose:** To remember it is God who gives all blessings

5. **Materials needed**

   a. Very light green background

   b. Metallic paper for holly, berries, and candles; foil Christmas wrapping paper is good

   c. Black construction paper or yarn for cursive letters

   d. Patterns for candles, berries, holly, and letters

* **Variations**

   a. Try Reynolds Wrap for the background

   b. Use green holly, red berries, yellow-green or white candles decorated with glitter

1. **New Year:** "Ring In the New Year"

2. **Source:** New Year of the calendar year; a famous saying

3. **Special emphasis:** Our relationship with God and others

4. **Aim or purpose:** To develop the concept that as Christians we put Jesus first in our lives, then others, and finally ourselves

5. **Materials needed**

   a. Light green background

   b. Bright green construction paper for the caption

   c. Heavy red yarn for "JOY" and bell cord

   d. White corrugated border

   e. Pattern and white construction paper for 10″ bells

   f. Red felt pen

* **Variations**

   a. Use white bells of styrofoam about one-half inch thick

   b. Make 1″ letters out of red paper and glue to the bells

   c. Make the letters for "JOY" out of metallic paper and mount on oak tag and attach to board with straight pins and pull out to heads of pins

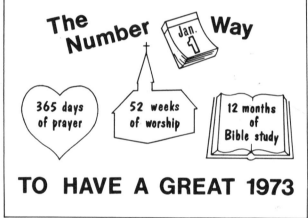

Patterns for 52 Visuals—see book list

1. **New Year:** "The Number 1 Way"

2. **Source:** New Year of the church year

3. **Special emphasis:** Spiritual growth in a new calendar year

4. **Aim or purpose:** To encourage spiritual growth through prayer, worship, and Bible study

5. **Materials needed**

   a. Yellow corrugated paper for background

   b. Red letters for "The Number" and "Way"

   c. Small box for "Jan. 1"

   d. Large white cutouts of heart, church, and Bible; red or black mounts

   e. Black letters for "TO HAVE A GREAT 1973"

   f. Black or red felt pen

1. **Missions:** "God Made People Different"

2. **Source:** John 3:16

3. **Special emphasis:** Even though people are different in many ways, God loves them all and wants them to be saved.

4. **Aim or purpose:** To discuss the differences of the peoples of the world, but to remember that God loves all people and sent His Son to die for all

5. **Materials needed**
   a. Light blue burlap, construction paper, or shelf paper for background
   b. Black construction paper for letters
   c. A world, about 12″ to 14″, either with continents or in abstract design with longitude and latitude lines
   d. Silhouettes of children, four to six pairs, of different sizes and colors such as white, natural, light and dark brown, red and brick red, yellow, or black
   e. Patterns for world, boy, and girl

* **Variations**
   a. You may arrange children in a single row around the board
   b. *Or* have a family group in each corner

---

1. **Missions:** "We Are Fishers of Men"

2. **Source:** The song "Fishers of Men"; Mark 1:14-19

3. **Special emphasis:** Encouraging children to bring friends or unchurched to Sunday school

4. **Aim or purpose:** To encourage children to bring their unchurched friends, classmates, or neighbors to Sunday school. The center fish with cross is to be used to teach how Jesus told His disciples that they should follow Him and He would make them fishers of men.

   When a guest is brought to church, weekday school, or Sunday school, the guest's name is written on a fish with the name of the child who brought him. If you wish, have a contest and give a little gift for the best fisherman

5. **Materials needed**
   a. Blue and green variegated tissue wrapping paper for the background, using the horizontal pattern to simulate waves
   b. Very light blue or light green construction paper for fish of different sizes
   c. White construction paper for letters and the fish with cross

* **Variations**
   a. Make a fishing net of net material, or just staple netting over the tissue paper
   b. If you wish, with light beige paper add banks at each end, and use a title like "Catching People for Jesus"
   c. Try a yellow for the caption and some of the fish

1. **Missions:** "Stop to Learn About God's Love"

2. **Source:** 1 John 4:7-11; 1 Peter 3:15

3. **Special emphasis:** Learning and sharing the Good News of God's love

4. **Aim or purpose:** To encourage Christians to learn God's Word accurately so they can be prepared and ready to witness whenever the opportunity arises

5. **Materials needed**
   a. White background
   b. Red construction paper for light and letters for "Stop"
   c. Green construction paper for light and letters for "Go"
   d. Black construction paper for other letters and the traffic light
   e. A large box about 10"×20"×1" deep
   f. *Or* a piece of black poster board about 12"×20" for the traffic light
   g. A pattern for the traffic light
   h. A picture of a class at church, mounted on red, *and* a picture of children at play, in school, or anywhere we can tell of God's love, mounted on green

   Note: Cover the box with the black construction paper, add red and green circle, staple bottom of box to board, add covered lid, and reinforce with long straight pins. If poster board is used, pull out to heads of pins

1. **Missions:** "Ears for Brazil"

2. **Source:** District Hearts for Jesus project

3. **Special emphasis:** Our Hearts for Jesus project to provide equipment for a deaf school in Brazil

4. **Aim or purpose:** To inform and promote our Hearts for Jesus project, which is to buy teaching and student equipment for a school for the deaf in Brazil

5. **Materials needed**

    a. Gold or aqua burlap for background
    b. Bright red, black, or yellow letters
    c. Three white hearts, 10″ to 12″
    d. Pictures of project equipment, such as typewriter, sewing machine, station wagon, mounted on hearts
    e. Black border such as corrugated Bordette

* **Variations**

    a. For older children add some facts about our mission work in Brazil
    b. For smaller children add a few word pictures of sign language

    Note: You may use this board for any mission project; just change the words and pictures

1. **Missions:** "Come, Lord Jesus, Be Our Guest"

2. **Source:** John 10:16

3. **Special emphasis:** Many people in foreign lands and in our own country want Jesus to come in their homes and live in their hearts. Jesus wants these people in His kingdom too

4. **Aim or purpose:** To remind children that there are many homes in the world where Jesus is not a guest as yet. He wants those people brought into His kingdom too. We must help make this possible through our mission work

5. **Materials needed**

    a. Yellow shelf paper or construction paper for the background
    b. Black and red letters
    c. Cutouts of homes of different countries, including your community
    d. Pattern or reference books for homes; add children with homes

   a. Have children collect items from those countries and have a table display in front of the bulletin board
   b. You may want to use pictures of one country, such as Argentina or Venezuela, instead of the world. This is especially true for older children, stressing that there are never enough workers for the many people who still need to hear about Jesus

---

C. Lent—Palm Sunday—Good Friday

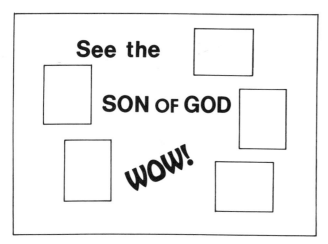 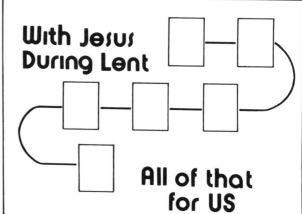

1. **Pre-Lent:** "See the Son of God"
2. **Source:** Pre-Lent of the church year; life of Christ, especially His miracles—His divine nature
3. **Special emphasis:** The miracles of Jesus—His divine nature
4. **Aim or purpose:** To instill in the children the power of Jesus and to show how He used it to help those who asked for help
5. **Materials needed**
   a. Light yellow background such as shelf paper or burlap
   b. Bright purple or magenta for letters (corrugated paper would be good for these) and red for "WOW!"
   c. White construction paper for picture mounts
   d. Pictures showing miracles of Jesus' power

---

1. **Lent:** "With Jesus During Lent"
2. **Source:** Lent of the church year
3. **Special emphasis:** The suffering and death of Jesus

4. **Aim or purpose:** To acquaint children with the Passion story through the use of pictures

5. **Materials needed**

   a. Black background

   b. White construction paper for picture mounts and letters in the top caption and the word "that" in the lower caption

   c. Red construction paper for lower caption letters

   d. Red yarn for strips

   e. Pictures from bulletins or Primary Sunday school leaflets

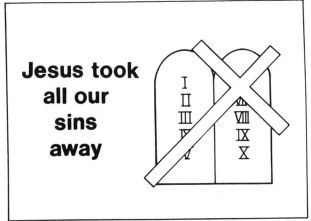 

Weekday

1. **Lent:** "Jesus Took All Our Sins Away"

2. **Source:** Lent of the church year; study of the Ten Commandments

3. **Special emphasis:** Jesus took all our sins away

4. **Aim or purpose:** To remind children of the purpose of Jesus' suffering and death, and to use the cross as an opportunity to bring in the Gospel when studying the Commandments

5. **Materials needed**

   a. Light beige or white corrugated paper or construction paper for the background

   b. Dark brown for letters

   c. Red construction paper for "all," "away," and the cross

   d. Tan or light brown paper for table of stone

   e. Pattern for table of stone and cross

   f. Black felt pen

* **Variations**

   a. Several shades of gray are good

   b. The cross could also be made out of red corrugated paper

---

1. **Lent:** "Look, Here Is the Man Jesus"

2. **Source:** Lent of the church year; Second Article, "suffered . . . crucified, dead, and buried"; "true man, born of the Virgin Mary"

3. **Special emphasis:** The suffering and death of Jesus

4. **Aim or purpose:** To review the accounts of the suffering and death of Jesus through the use of pictures

5. **Materials needed**
   a. Light lavender or violet background
   b. Red construction paper for letters for "LOOK" and "JESUS"
   c. Black construction paper for rest of the letters in the caption
   d. Pictures showing the suffering and death of Jesus on white mounts

* **Variations**
   a. If you wish, use the wording "Behold the Man" (John 19:5 KJV)
   b. A beige or black background with contrasting letters would be good
   c. Capital letters, 4" or larger

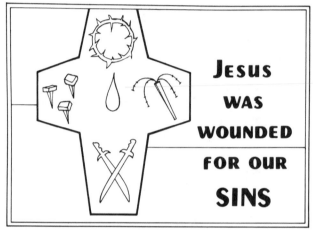

Sacred design

1. **Lent—Good Friday:** "Jesus Was Wounded for Our Sins"

2. **Source:** Isaiah 53:5; Luke 23

3. **Special emphasis:** The suffering and death of Jesus our Savior for our sins

4. **Aim or purpose:** To study the prophecy in Isaiah 53 concerning the suffering and death of Jesus and its fulfillment as recorded in Luke 23

5. **Materials needed**
   a. Light gray corrugated paper for the background
   b. Medium gray for lower part of board
   c. Dark gray for large cross, 20"×30"
   d. Red construction paper for drop of blood, letters for "wounded," and 2" border
   e. Black construction paper for letters for "Jesus was" and for cutouts on cross
   f. White construction paper for letters "for our SINS"
   g. Black yarn, nails, and stick for scourge

* **Variations**
   a. You may use the stencils entitled "The Story of Jesus" on the cross instead of the other cutouts; make them in black (see list of resources)
   b. Leave the red drop of blood to show that Jesus' death and suffering were slow and painful

1. **Palm Sunday:** "The Children Sang Hosanna!"

2. **Source:** Palm Sunday of the church year; Jesus' entry into Jerusalem; Matt. 21:15-16

3. **Special emphasis:** The children singing "Hosanna," praise to the Lord

4. **Aim or purpose:** To encourage children to praise God because Jesus Himself said theirs was perfect praise

5. **Materials needed**
   a. Pink background; burlap or construction paper would be best
   b. Pattern and purple construction paper for Chi-Rho and border
   c. Palm branches from the florist
   d. White, green, or black construction paper for the letters

* **Variations**
   a. You could have a lovely board by using a chartreuse background, a purple border and Chi-Rho, and magenta or bright rose letters
   b. Palm branches may be made of green construction paper
   c. If you wish to pull the Chi-Rho out to the heads of pins, you will need to glue it to heavy paper for more body; then place the palm branches behind it

---

1. **Palm Sunday:** "Palm Sunday"

2. **Source:** Holy Week of the church year; Jesus' entry into Jerusalem

3. **Special emphasis:** Jesus' entry into Jerusalem and other activities prior to His suffering and death

4. **Aim or purpose:** To study the events of Holy Week prior to Jesus' captivity

5. **Materials needed**
   a. Light yellow background
   b. Palm branches from the florists
   c. Gold metallic paper for the crown
   d. Purple construction paper or metallic paper for the letters
   e. Straight pins for letters and crown
   f. Pictures of Jesus' activities and teachings during Holy Week, such as His entry into Jerusalem, the cleansing of the temple, the widow's mite, the ten virgins, and the institution of the Lord's Supper

1. **Palm Sunday:** "Crown Him Lord of All"

2. **Source:** Palm Sunday of the church year; "Crown Him with Many Crowns," *The Lutheran Hymnal,* No. 341; "All Hail the Power of Jesus' Name," *The Lutheran Hymnal,* No. 339

3. **Special emphasis:** Jesus' entry into Jerusalem on Palm Sunday for Holy Week; world missions

4. **Aim or purpose**
   a. To study Jesus' activities during Holy Week before His captivity
   b. To emphasize that Jesus is the Lord of all nations and came to save all

5. **Materials needed**
   a. White, light yellow, or lavender burlap for the background
   b. Gold metallic paper for the crown
   c. Black construction or corrugated paper for the cross and orb
   d. Stiff cardboard for backing of cross and orb
   e. Small ½" pieces of styrofoam
   f. Palm branches from a floral shop or made by the children
   g. Black construction paper for letters
   h. Pictures of Jesus' activities during Holy Week, mounted on light green or white; or pictures of our mission work in foreign countries

Crown Him Lord of All

Truly this Man was the Son of God

Bulletin A. P. H.

1. **Good Friday:** "Truly This Man Was the Son of God"

2. **Source:** Holy Week of the church year; the Second Article, "true God, Son of the Father from eternity"

3. **Special emphasis:** The suffering and death of Jesus

4. **Aim or purpose:** To recall with pictures the events of our Savior's suffering and death and to remember that He who did this for us was the Son of God

5. **Materials needed**
   a. Black background
   b. Patterns and white construction paper for 4" capital letters
   c. Red construction paper for small letters
   d. Two large or four small pictures of the suffering and death of Jesus, mounted on white

   a. Beige (sand) corrugated paper for background
   b. Red and black letters

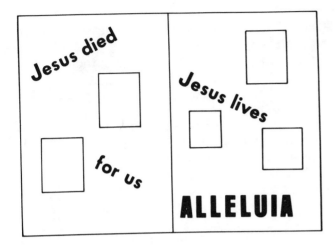

1. **Good Friday—Easter:** "Jesus Died, Jesus Lives"
2. **Source:** Holy Week of the church year; the Second Article, "suffered . . . was crucified, dead, and buried" and "the third day He rose again from the dead"
3. **Special emphasis:** The suffering, death, and resurrection of Jesus
4. **Aim or purpose:** To teach with pictures the events of Jesus' suffering, death, and resurrection
5. **Materials needed**
   a. Purple for left half and bright green for right half of board for the background (corrugated or construction paper are best)
   b. Black letters for "Jesus died for us"
   c. White letters for "Jesus lives"
   d. Yellow letters for "ALLELUIA," banner style
   e. Pictures of Jesus' suffering and death on dark mounts
   f. Pictures of Jesus' resurrection and postresurrection appearances on white or yellow mounts

D. Easter—Ascension—Pentecost

1. **Easter:** "Jesus Lives, Alleluia"
2. **Source:** Easter of the church year; the Second Article

3. **Special emphasis:** The resurrection of Jesus; the Second Article, "on the third day He rose again from the dead"

4. **Aim or purpose:** A visual aid to strengthen the concept that Jesus appeared to various people in proof of His resurrection

5. **Materials needed**

   a. Bright green background of burlap, corrugated or construction paper
   b. Bright yellow construction paper for letters
   c. Black tagboard or heavy construction paper for the triptych and Chi-Rho
   d. Picture of empty tomb (if none is available, make a design of stone rolled away to show empty tomb)
   e. Pictures of Jesus' appearances after His resurrection
   f. White paper for decorative design, picture mount, and angels
   g. Patterns for angels, Chi-Rho, and letters

How series

1. **Post-Easter:** "My Redeemer Lives"
2. **Source:** Easter of the church year; "I Know that My Redeemer Lives," *The Lutheran Hymnal,* No. 200
3. **Special emphasis:** Jesus' resurrection
4. **Aim or purpose:** To make a collage while studying the Scriptural accounts of the post-Easter appearances of Jesus
5. **Materials needed**

   a. Construction paper for the sky, ground, and path for the background
   b. Bright pink or rose for letters (corrugated paper would be good)
   c. Rock design paper, either corrugated or wallpaper, for the grave, or gray paper to make rock design; gray paper for the stone in front of the grave
   d. Sticks, rocks, cotton, etc., to put on the background

* **Variations**

   You may use dark gray construction paper for the grave; crumple the paper, then straighten it out somewhat and staple it to the board, leaving a rounded effect

1. **Ascension:** ''And You Also Are Witnesses''

2. **Source:** Ascension Day in the church year

3. **Special emphasis:** Missions, as in the Ascension account in Acts 1:8, where Jesus commands His disciples to witness in Jerusalem, Judea, Samaria, and to the end of the earth

4. **Aim or purpose:** To motivate witnessing in the neighborhood, city, state, throughout the country, for evangelism

5. **Materials needed**

   a. Bright purple for background
   b. Bright yellow construction paper or heavy yarn for cursive letters
   c. Pictures of places to witness, brought by children or yourself and mounted on white
   d. White silhouettes of a family and a silhouette of Jesus

Sacred design   Sacred design

1. **Ascension:** ''Teaching Them All That I Have Commanded You''

2. **Source:** Ascension Day of the church year; Matt. 28:19-20

3. **Special emphasis:** Christian education, missions, the story of Jesus' ascension into heaven

4. **Aim or purpose:** To teach the command of Jesus that we make disciples of all people, and His promise to send His Holy Spirit to help us

5. **Materials needed**

   a. Orange and brown construction paper for the background
   b. Black corrugated or construction paper for the shepherd's crook (a symbol of Jesus)
   c. White corrugated paper, construction paper, felt, or art pellon for the dove
   d. Bright orange paper for letters
   e. Pattern for dove and shepherd's crook

1. **Pentecost:** ''Holy Spirit, Come and Teach Us''

2. **Source:** Pentecost of the church year; the Third Article, ''The Holy Spirit has called me through the Gospel''; unit on the Bible

3. **Special emphasis:** The work of the Holy Spirit

4. **Aim or purpose:** An activity to teach the concept that the Holy Spirit uses God's Word to teach us and makes our faith grow

5. **Materials needed**
   a. Black background
   b. White paper for dove and the letters
   c. Red or red-orange construction paper for flames
   d. Black felt pen
   e. Pattern for dove and flame

Bible references for the flames

| Matt. 28:19 | 1 Cor. 12:3 | 1 Cor. 2:13 | Titus 3:5 | John 14:26 |
| John 3:5-6 | Rom. 15:13 | 1 Cor. 2:10 | Acts 7:51 | 1 Cor. 3:16 |

1. **Pentecost:** "Pentecost, the Birthday of the Christian Church"

2. **Source:** Pentecost of the Church Year, Acts 2; the Third Article

3. **Special emphasis:** The beginning of the early Christian church and the work of the Holy Spirit in the Third Article

4. **Aim or purpose:** To establish time and event of the beginning of the early Christian church

5. **Materials needed**
   a. Light blue or aqua background
   b. Pattern and white pellon or construction paper for the dove, about 16″ long
   c. Red or red-orange cellophane, metallic paper, or construction paper for the flames
   d. Heavy red yarn for "Pentecost"
   e. Red construction paper for "Birthday" and "Christian Church"
   f. Black construction paper for lowercase words

---

1. **Post-Pentecost:** "Fruits of the Spirit"

2. **Source:** Pentecost of the church year; Gal. 5:22-23

3. **Special emphasis:** The fruits of the Holy Spirit, a study of the Third Article, and Christian character

34

4. **Aim or purpose:** To teach the fruits of the work of the Holy Spirit and to consider when we can make good use of these Christian characteristics

5. **Materials needed**
   a. White background
   b. Lavender and purple construction paper for the circles, 3″ to 4″ in diameter
   c. Patterns and green construction paper for leaves
   d. Black for letters, green for Scripture verse
   e. Purple border
   f. Black felt pen

E. Trinity

1. **Trinity:** "Father, Son, and Holy Spirit"

2. **Source:** Trinity Sunday of the church year; the Apostles' Creed

3. **Special emphasis:** The triune God; the work of creation, redemption, and sanctification

4. **Aim or purpose:** To introduce a study of the Trinity and the Apostles' Creed and to study some of the basic symbols used to describe the Godhead

5. **Materials needed**
   a. A yellow-green or light green burlap or felt for the background
   b. Strips of white paper, 2″ wide, to divide board into three parts
   c. Bright red letters for "Father," "Son," and "Holy Spirit," odd sizes
   d. Capital letters, 2″ high, and bright green paper for "CREATOR," "REDEEMER," and "COMFORTER"
   e. Patterns for symbols and black corrugated or construction paper

Sacred design

1. **Trinity:** "Blessed Trinity, Alleluia"

2. **Source:** Trinity Sunday of the church year; the Apostles' Creed; Mark 1:9-11

3. **Special emphasis:** Praising the Trinity

4. **Aim or purpose:** To use the account of Jesus' baptism to introduce the Trinity and to praise God for His threefold work

5. **Materials needed**
   a. Bright green construction paper for background
   b. Black construction paper for cross and letters
   c. Pattern for 9″ to 10″ triangles and yellow-green corrugated paper for the 3 triangles
   d. White paper and patterns for symbols
   e. A picture of Jesus' baptism with dove descending, mounted on black or white
   f. Pattern for cross about 3″ wide and full length of board

F. Reformation

1. **Reformation:** "Luther's Great Discovery in Scriptures"

2. **Source:** Reformation of the church year; Eph. 2:8; the weekday course *Luther, Servant of God*

3. **Special emphasis:** "Saved by Grace," the central truth of the Reformation

4. **Aim or purpose:** To develop the concept that "we are saved by grace through faith," which was the central truth of the Reformation and has been the central teaching of the Lutheran Church

5. **Materials needed**

   a. Black construction paper for background, Bible, cross
   b. Yellow construction paper for stream of heavenly light
   c. Red construction paper for caption letters and heart
   d. White paper for Scripture verse
   e. Red felt pen
   f. Pattern for open Bible, about 12" to 14"

* **Variations**

   a. You may want to use liquid embroidery and make the Bible out of art pellon. Artex has a large Bible transfer that works nicely
   b. You can add variety to this design by adding yellow cellophane to the stream of light

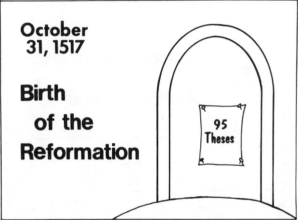

1. **Reformation:** "Birth of the Reformation"

2. **Source:** Reformation of the church year

3. **Special emphasis:** The Ninety-Five Theses

4. **Aim or purpose:** To establish the date and occasion of the beginning of the Reformation and to become acquainted with some of the more important theses

5. **Materials needed**

   a. Light green or light yellow for background
   b. Wallpaper paneling or brown construction paper for the door
   c. Dark brown construction paper for door frame
   d. White sheet of paper for "95 Theses"
   e. Thumbtacks to tack theses to door
   f. Green construction paper for date
   g. Red construction paper for caption letters
   h. Door pattern and letter patterns

1. **Reformation:** "Luther, Servant of God"

2. **Source:** Reformation of the church year; the weekday course *Luther, Servant of God*

3. **Special emphasis:** Major events of the Reformation, such as the Diet of Worms

4. **Aim or purpose:** To acquaint children with the great events of the Reformation through the use of pictures

5. **Materials needed**
   a. White background of burlap or corrugated paper
   b. Red, black, or brown for letters and border
   c. Different-sized pictures (old *This Day* magazines and various religious art calendars can provide these)
   d. Letter patterns
   e. Construction paper for picture mounts

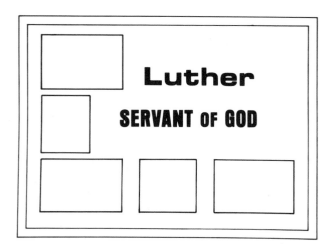

1. **Reformation:** "Luther, Man of God"

2. **Source:** Reformation of the church year; the weekday course *Luther, Servant of God*

3. **Special emphasis:** Luther seal, Luther's work as musician, translator, and educator

4. **Aim or purpose:** To introduce a study of the Luther seal and its meaning and to learn of Luther's contributions in music, translation of the Bible, and education

5. **Materials needed**
   a. White, light tan, or natural for background
   b. Pattern for special picture mounts
   c. Black or brown construction paper or corrugated paper for mounts
   d. Red construction paper for letters
   e. Luther seal or a large picture of one
   f. A devotion for the study of the Luther seal
   g. Pictures showing Luther as translator, teacher, or musician

G. Thanksgiving

1. **Thanksgiving:** "Thanks Be to God"

2. **Source:** Thanksgiving of the church year; the life of Christ, especially His miracles

3. **Special emphasis:** Giving thanks for the power Jesus has as God's Son

4. **Aim or purpose:** To develop an awareness of the blessings of God's power

5. **Materials needed**
   a. Yellow or white corrugated paper for the background
   b. Brown construction paper for letters and picture mounts
   c. Letter patterns in several sizes and special pattern for the "T"
   d. Pictures showing some of the miracles of Jesus

* **Variations** (for life of Christ)
   a. Use shades of purple and reds for the background
   b. Use contrasting color or white for the letters

1. **Thanksgiving:** "Thank You, God, for Everything"

2. **Source:** Thanksgiving of the church year

3. **Special emphasis:** Giving thanks for everything

4. **Aim or purpose:** To give thanks for everything we receive from God

5. **Materials needed**
   a. Aqua corrugated paper or burlap (light blue is pretty too)
   b. Brown and orange construction paper for letters and double-mount cross
   c. Hallmark decorations, or have children make the fruits and vegetables

1. **Thanksgiving:** "Thank God for His Son"

2. **Source:** Thanksgiving of the church year; Lent of the church year

3. **Special emphasis:** Jesus submitted to His Father's plan of salvation

4. **Aim or purpose:** Thankfulness that Jesus kept His goal of dying on the cross for all people

5. **Materials needed**
   a. Dark brown construction paper or wallpaper paneling for background
   b. A picture of an empty cross and a picture of Jesus looking to the cross
   c. Bright yellow for letters
   d. Corrugated border in white, or make your own border
   e. White construction paper or corrugated paper for picture mounts

* **Variations** (for the Lenten season)
   a. Use a gray background
   b. Red paper for letters
   c. White paper for picture mounts
   d. Use a black border

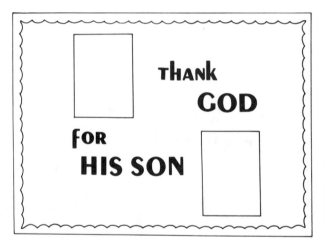 

Sacred Design

1. **Thanksgiving:** "In All Things Giving Thanks and Praise"

2. **Source:** Thanksgiving of the church year; prayer or Second Commandment

3. **Special emphasis:** Giving thanks for all things

4. **Aim or purpose:** To motivate the viewers to give thanks and praise to God in all things and to learn to make such prayers

5. **Materials needed**
   a. For the background, large sheets of construction paper in four colors such as gold, green, brown, orange, tan, or yellow
   b. White construction paper for praying hands, strips to form cross, and letters
   c. Praying hands and letter patterns

* **Variations** (for prayer or Second Commandment)

   a. Different shades of blue and green for the background
   b. Black paper for cross and letters
   c. Pictures showing things we will want to pray for or blessings we thank
   God for

1. **Thanksgiving:** "Give Thanks unto the Lord"

2. **Source:** Thanksgiving of the church year

3. **Special emphasis:** Giving thanks for home, school, and country (social
   needs)

4. **Aim or purpose:** To make a prayer of thanksgiving for our home, school,
   and country

5. **Materials needed**

   a. Light blue or aqua burlap for the background
   b. Orange and brown construction paper for letters and double mount
   cross
   c. Patterns and white construction paper or art pellon for Pilgrim hats
   (or try felt)
   d. Black and red felt pens or liquid embroidery
   e. Leaves gathered by children, or Hallmark or Dennison prints of leaves

* **Variations** (for physical needs)

   a. May use large pumpkins, about 9″ to 10″, instead of the hats
   b. Use words such as food, clothing, house, good health
   c. Have children make leaves out of construction paper
   d. You may add a border of corrugated paper instead of folding edges
   of burlap under

PART III
Bulletin Boards Showing
              God's Gifts to Us

A. The Ten Commandments—
Christian Growth and Worship

1. **The Ten Commandments:** "God's Rules for Happy Living"
2. **Source:** The Ten Commandments
3. **Special emphasis:** God's rules were given as a guide for God-pleasing living for the whole family
4. **Aim or purpose:** To study and memorize the Ten Commandments, God's guide for happy living for the whole family
5. **Materials needed**
   a. Green for grass, gray or beige for road on background
   b. Black letters
   c. Cutouts of man, woman, boy, and girl
   d. Ten shapes similar to the traffic signs common to your locality; write a commandment on each sign
   e. Mounts for the traffic signs, leaving about one-fourth inch on all sides
* **Variations**
   a. Use a plain background
   b. Put caption in center of board and arrange signs in order around the outside, from the top left corner to the right, down, left, and up. Have a small vehicle for each child to place his name on and park by the commandment he has memorized
   c. You may also make a small version of the design, give each child a page, and have the children color each sign as they memorize the commandment

1. **The Commandments:** "God's Law for a Happy Life"
2. **Source:** The Ten Commandments
3. **Special emphasis:** God gave His law so we would have some guides for a happy life

4. **Aim or purpose:** To motivate children to live a happy life by submitting to God's law

5. **Materials needed**
   a. Yellow shelf paper or construction paper for the background
   b. Blue-green construction paper for the letters
   c. Light tan or gray construction paper for the tables of stone
   d. Pictures showing positive phase of the commandments, adding one or two at a time; or one picture of Moses and the tables of stone
   e. Pattern for table of stone (Artex has a good pattern and also a large pattern of Moses and the tables of stone)
   f. Felt pen for the Roman numerals

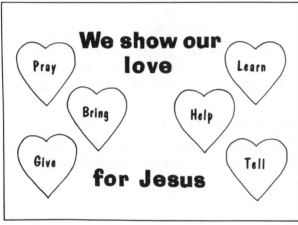

Weekday

1. **The Commandments:** "We Show Our Love for Jesus"

2. **Source:** The First Commandment: "love . . . God above anything else"; the First Article: "Therefore I surely ought to thank and praise, serve and obey Him"

3. **Special emphasis:** Showing love for Jesus by serving Him

4. **Aim or purpose:** To show children the many ways they can serve God.

5. **Materials needed**
   a. Light green background
   b. Blue-green letters
   c. Red hearts, 8" to 9", for mounts
   d. Line drawings on white hearts showing activities of children serving God
   e. Religious coloring books for line drawings; or if time is available, have children do the drawing
   f. Felt pens for drawings

* **Variations**
   a. For the older children make a large heart about 24"×24" and arrange pictures in a montage
   b. Use a 2" letter and include it on the heart
   c. Cover hearts with red cellophane and omit red mounts

45

1. **The Commandments:** "Why God Gave Us His Word"

2. **Source:** The Third Commandment; 2 Tim. 1:1-5; 3:14-17; Ps. 199:105; in *The Lutheran Hymnal,* "How Precious Is the Book Divine," No. 285; "How Shall the Young Secure Their Hearts," No. 286; and "Blessed Jesus, at Thy Word," No. 16

3. **Special emphasis:** The purpose of the Holy Scriptures

4. **Aim or purpose:** To teach the concept that God gave us His Word so we could learn of our salvation through His Son Jesus and of God's guide for our everyday living

5. **Materials needed**
   a. Light yellow background
   b. Black construction paper, 18"×24"
   c. White construction paper, 18"×24"
   d. Red felt pen to make page lines of Bible, black felt pen for words on Bible
   e. Light brown or tan construction paper for cross and table of stone
   f. Red letters for caption
   g. Make a large pattern for open Bible out of newspaper according to size of your board
   Note: When attaching the Bible to the board, staple first on the center line, then bring in side edges of white about 1" so you get 3-D effect of an open Bible

---

1. **The Commandments:** "Remember Time for VBS"

2. **Source:** The Third Commandment, "gladly hear and learn God's Word"

3. **Special emphasis:** Date and time of the first VBS class

4. **Aim or purpose:** To remind people of the time and date of VBS; can be used for any event to be remembered

5. **Materials needed**
   a. Aqua background
   b. Red and black letters
   c. White paper and pattern for the clock
   d. Bright yellow for mount for clock
   e. Red, blue, aqua, and black felt pens to draw facial features on the clock

1. **The Commandments:** "God Says, Honor Your Mother and Father"

2. **Source:** The Fourth Commandment; Mother's and Father's Day; unit on the family

3. **Special emphasis:** Honoring mothers and fathers

4. **Aim or purpose:** To illustrate ways children can honor their parents, such as helping with work, writing letters home when away, giving them gifts, caring for them when they are ill, obeying them, respectfully listening to God's Word, and calling them on the phone

5. **Materials needed**
   a. Light blue background
   b. Dark blue and red letters in different sizes
   c. Pictures showing ways to honor parents
   d. Blue, white, or red construction paper for picture mounts

* **Variations**
   a. Can be used with other themes such as "Love One Another" or "Pray for Each Other"
   b. Liquid embroidery companies have good patterns for cutouts to add interest to this board

 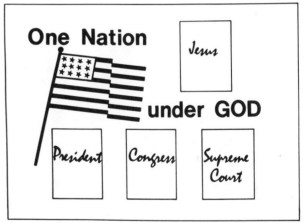

1. **The Commandments:** "One Nation Under God"

2. **Source:** The Fourth Commandment; pledge of allegiance to the U. S. flag

3. **Special emphasis:** Our country is directed by God through the three branches of government

4. **Aim or purpose:** To develop the concept that our country is directed by God through the three branches of government and that we should respect and obey our government

5. **Materials needed**
   a. Light blue or white background
   b. Bright red or red-orange for letters
   c. A cutout of our flag or a small flag
   d. One picture each of Jesus and of the President, Congress, and Supreme Court

* **Variations**

    a. Use a bright blue for background

    b. White letters and picture mounts

    c. You may divide the background in three equal parts of red, white, and blue

    d. Use contrasting letters such as red on blue, blue on white, and white on red, or use all black letters

    Note: Be sure to place "under God" directly under the picture of Jesus for the small children

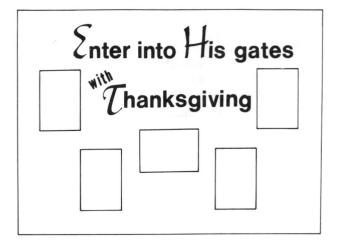

1. **Worship:** "Enter into His Gates with Thanksgiving"

2. **Source:** The Third Commandment, "gladly hear and learn God's Word"; the First Article, "I ought to thank and praise Him"; Psalm 100:4

3. **Special emphasis:** Churches come in different styles; we should enter all of them with a thankful heart for the many blessings we receive from God

4. **Aim or purpose:** To give children an opportunity to discuss the various styles of churches they have worshiped in and to be reminded that we go to church to worship God with a thankful heart

5. **Materials needed**

    a. Use a yellow-green background

    b. Brown letters and orange capitals or orange letters for the words "His" and "Thanksgiving"

    c. Pictures of church interiors

    d. Brown or beige mounts for pictures

    e. Letter patterns for the E, H, and T

* **Variations**

    a. Make this board more personal by adding some small symbols that are found in your church, such as a special cross, altar, or pulpit symbol

    b. Liturgical colors are appropriate for this design

1. **Worship:** "Come, Let Us Worship the Lord"

2. **Source:** The Third Commandment, "do not neglect His Word or the preaching of it"

3. **Special emphasis:** Invitation to come to worship

4. **Aim or purpose:** To invite and encourage regular worship

5. **Materials needed**
   a. Light green shelf paper for the background
   b. Purple letters, some words in larger capitals and others in smaller
   c. Pictures of churches, in different sizes and styles if possible, and some with people on them
   d. White and different shades of purple for picture mounts
   e. Bright green or black border

* **Variations**
   a. Add interest to this board by including a cutout of some special feature of the exterior of your church, such as a certain style of cross or door, or make a small replica of your church sign with the name of your church out of construction paper
   b. You can use seasonal colors instead of green and purple
   c. This theme can be made into a lovely Christmas board: include churches decorated for the holidays; make a border of holly leaves and berries, or use pine branches

 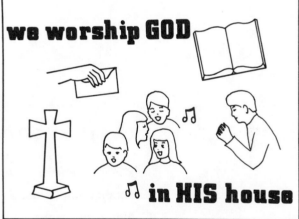

1. **Worship:** "We Worship God in HIS House"
2. **Source:** The Third Commandment "gladly hear and learn God's Word;" the Second Article, "For all which it is my duty to thank and praise Him"

3. **Special emphasis:** The different activities of the church service

4. **Aim or purpose:** To encourage proper understanding of the parts or acts of worship; use the cross to remind us that our motivation for worship should be what Jesus has done for us.

5. **Materials needed**
   a. Use a light yellow or light green for the background
   b. Bright green, blue-green, or blue for the letters, some capitals and some lowercase

c. Cutout patterns from coloring books on worship

d. *Or* pictures showing worship activities

* **Variations**

   a. You may use shades and tints of the liturgical color being used in church

   b. Include pictures of all ages and illustrate activities in your own services

---

B. The Apostles' Creed

1. **The Articles:** "God Made Us; We Can Praise Him"

2. **Source:** The First Article: "God the Father . . . Maker of heaven and earth" and "I surely ought to thank and praise, serve and obey Him"

3. **Special emphasis:** Praising God for the work of creation

4. **Aim or purpose:** To lead children to praise God for creating man and the animals and to realize man is the only creature equipped to praise God

5. **Materials needed**

   a. White or light yellow background

   b. Construction paper for silhouettes the color of animals

   c. Black construction paper for silhouettes of the children

   d. Construction paper for balloon cutouts for the captions

   e. Black felt pen to print letters

   f. Pattern book for animals and children

* **Variations**

   a. Green for grass and light blue for sky in background

   b. You may also use the Hallmark packet of animals

   c. Have an animal for each student and give each a seal to put on his animal for memory work learned each week

 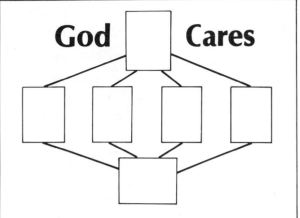

1. **The Articles:** "God Gives Me All I Need"

2. **Source:** The First Article, "He provides me with food and clothing . . ."; the Fourth Petition, "Give us this day our daily bread"

3. **Special emphasis:** God provides me with all I need

4. **Aim or purpose:** To make a montage showing all the blessings God provides us.

5. **Materials needed**

   a. Light yellow, green, blue, or pink background
   b. Bright letters in different sizes
   c. Pictures, brought by children, of the things God provides

* **Variations**

   a. For smaller children, ditto cutouts of food, clothing, home, school, church, money; or let them draw or cut out their own
   b. With three or four good pictures illustrate the blessings God gives, and use a formal arrangement
   c. Use doll clothes to represent our clothing, form a three-dimensional home and church about 1″ deep out of construction paper, make an open Bible, and put up some plastic toy food. Be sure to attach them to the board securely, for small children like to "feel" things

---

1. **The Articles:** "God cares"

2. **Source:** The First Article, "provides me with . . . all I need from day to day"

3. **Special emphasis:** God uses certain people as His instruments in taking care of us

4. **Aim or purpose:** To teach that God preserves us, or takes care of us, through our parents, teachers, pastor, and other community helpers such as doctors, nurses, and policemen

5. **Materials needed**

   a. Light blue, light green, or aqua for background
   b. Bright blue or green for letters and yarn
   c. A picture of Jesus and a picture of a boy and girl
   d. Cutouts of community helpers

1. **The Articles:** "Look, God Made a Great World"

2. **Source:** Genesis 1; the First Article

3. **Special emphasis:** What God created was great

4. **Aim or purpose:** To make a collage showing some of the things God made when He created the world

5. **Materials needed**

   a. Construction paper for sky, lake, grass
   b. Brown wallpaper paneling or brown corrugated paper for tree trunk
   c. Green corrugated or construction paper for tree
   d. Animals, birds, fish, butterflies made by children (use patterns to save time), or use Hallmark animal decorations
   e. Cotton for clouds, Easter grass for the grass, small rocks or pebbles, etc.

* **Variations**

   a. Divide board into fourths and make a four-seasons board. Use 1" black strips to divide seasons; if your board is large enough, put a border around it
   b. If you wish, add one or two children in a seasonal activity
   c. This also works as the top of a calendar

   Note: This is a good board to have the children assist you in making

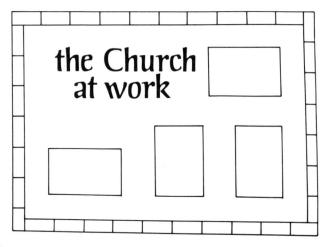

1. **The Articles:** "The Church at Work"

2. **Source:** The Third Article

3. **Special emphasis:** The work of the church with Word and sacrament, witness, missions, education

4. **Aim or purpose:** To discuss the work of the church, such as administering the sacraments, education, evangelism, missions

5. **Materials needed**

   a. Brick red burlap for background
   b. White brick design for the border
   c. White letters and picture mounts
   d. Pictures of types of work the people of the church do: evangelism, education, foreign missions, administering the sacraments

   Note: Bulletins are very good to illustrate this theme

a. White background
b. Red brick corrugated paper for border
c. Black letters
d. Black and red picture mounts
e. To make the board more personal, use a theme such as "God's People at Work," "Our Church at Work," or include the name of your church, "Peace at Work"
f. Any color of brick is appropriate, especially the color of your church

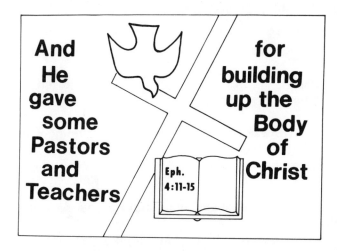

1. **The Articles:** "And He Gave Some Pastors and Teachers"

2. **Source:** Eph. 4:11-15; the Third Article, "the holy Christian church, the communion of saints"

3. **Special emphasis:** Jesus established the preaching and teaching ministry to build up (strengthen) the body of Christ

4. **Aim or purpose:** To teach the concept that Jesus established the preaching and teaching ministry to build up the body of believers

5. **Materials needed**
   a. Brick red burlap for the background
   b. Black construction paper for the cross and Bible
   c. Red 3″ letters for "and He gave some, the body of Christ"
   d. White construction paper for Bible pages and dove
   e. White 3″ letters for "Pastors and Teachers" and "for building up"
   f. Dove pattern, 13″ or 14″ high, and Bible pattern, about 10″×12″

* **Variations**
   a. Pin-back display letters are great for this board
   b. Use a bright yellow construction paper for the background
   c. Red and black letters
   d. Black art pellon for cross
   e. White art pellon for dove and Bible

   Note: When you are through with the cross, fold it for easy storage; iron it when you need it again

C. Lord's Prayer — Prayer and Praise

1. **The Lord's Prayer:** "Lord, Teach Us to Pray"

2. **Source:** Luke 11:1-4; Matt. 6:9-15

3. **Special emphasis:** The petitions of the Lord's Prayer

4. **Aim or purpose:** To introduce a study of the Lord's Prayer; to use the cross to remind us that Jesus taught us this prayer; and to remember that we pray to God the Father as His dear children

5. **Materials needed**

   a. A bright blue corrugated paper burlap or construction paper for background

   b. White construction paper for cross, hand of God, and the letters

   c. Light blue for silhouettes of boy and girl and for mount of hand and cross

   d. Blue or black felt pen to write petitions on silhouettes, beginning with top right figure and going clockwise

   e. Pattern for hand, cross, and silhouettes

* **Variations**

   a. This design may be used for teaching other prayers you want the children to memorize

   b. Have your class write their own prayers to pray with the class, make a silhouette for each child, and add them to the board as they fit in with your lessons

   c. You may wish to use different colors for this board, such as white for the boy and girl silhouettes, dark blue or black letters

   Note: You may use this idea for teaching the Apostles' Creed too. Use silhouettes of things created for the First Article, etc.

Sacred design

1. **Prayer:** "Hear My Prayer, O Lord"

2. **Source:** Prayer

3. **Special emphasis:** Asking God to hear our prayer

4. **Aim or purpose:** To use pictures to show various times when we will want and need to pray. For older children, change the pictures to illustrate different types of prayers. The cross reminds us that we should pray in Jesus' name

5. **Materials needed**
   a. White background of corrugated paper or burlap
   b. Bright brown construction paper or felt for central panel and side borders
   c. Two white circles 8″ to 9″ in diameter
   d. Silhouettes of cross and person
   e. Red-orange mount for cross
   f. Green mount for person
   g. Red-orange letters
   h. Pictures illustrating various needs we pray for, on red and green mounts.

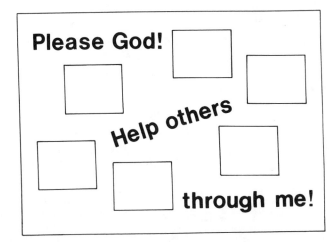

1. **Prayer:** "Please, God! Help Others Through Me!"

2. **Source:** Prayer of supplication

3. **Special emphasis:** A welfare project for needy persons whom we should pray for daily

4. **Aim or purpose:** To make a montage showing needy persons we should pray for, and to discuss ways we can help someone who needs assistance

5. **Materials needed**
   a. Any light background, perhaps with a free form of a contrasting color to mount pictures on
   b. Letters in bright colors such as red or blue-green, orange, yellow-green
   c. Pictures brought by children

* **Variations**
   a. Choose a few very good illustrations and arrange a more formal design
   b. Adapt the design for a mission activity, using a theme such as "Please, God! Help Me Tell Others About You." Use pictures of places where we may speak to others about God and His Word, and include times of danger as well as good times

1. **Prayer:** "It's Time to Talk to God"

2. **Source:** Unit on prayer

3. **Special emphasis:** Any time is a good time for prayer

4. **Aim or purpose:** To use pictures of daily activities to motivate children in grades 2—4 to write prayers appropriate for those activities. For older children, omit clockface and use activities common to their age level

5. **Materials needed**

   a. Green, blue, or aqua for background
   b. Bright yellow, orange, red, or pink for letters and clock mount
   c. Construction paper, white for 12″ clockface and black for hands
   d. Large paper fastener for hands
   e. Felt pen for numbers
   f. Small half-inch pieces of styrofoam to glue around circumference on back of clockface, to extend clock from board so hands move freely
   g. Pictures showing such scenes as play, study, school bus, meals, bedtime, going to church, vacation, etc.

   Note: Change hands to different times of day and have the children write a prayer concerning a common activity at each hour. Begin with an easy mealtime prayer. You may wish to have the children make booklets in the shape of a clock.

1. **Sacred music:** "Holy God, We Praise Thy Name"

2. **Source:** "Holy God, We Praise Thy Name," *The Lutheran Hymnal,* No. 250; the Second Commandment, "call on Him in prayer, praise, and thanksgiving."

3. **Special emphasis:** Different kinds of scared music and instruments used in church

4. **Aim or purpose:** To introduce a study of the kinds of music used in church and church schools, such as the organ, trumpets, guitars, bells, choirs, anthems, folk masses, etc. Ask your director of education and music, organist, or choir director to assist in this study with demonstrations, music, records, etc.

5. **Materials needed**
   a. Bright brown or tan corrugated paper, burlap, or construction paper for background
   b. Blue-green or aqua ribbon or paper cut in free form as mount for letters
   c. Dark brown letters
   d. Pictures showing choirs, organ, or special music on white mounts
   e. White notes for background
   f. Small instruments to staple to the background (check with your organist to find out which instruments your church organ simulates)

* **Variations**
   a. Put the caption on a banner
   b. Use liturgical colors for a Christmas or Easter board

1. **Sacred music:** "Sing a New Song"

2. **Source:** Psalm 33

3. **Special emphasis:** Learning new songs, praising God, and studying musical instruments of the Bible

4. **Aim or purpose**
   a. To use a psalm to motivate children to learn new songs in Sunday and weekday school
   b. To use the harp, a symbol of sacred music, to introduce a study or research of musical instruments common in the Bible

5. **Materials needed**
   a. Light green or light blue for the background
   b. Black construction paper for lowercase letters
   c. Patterns and red construction paper for special capital letters
   d. Cutouts of boy and girl, or pictures of children singing
   e. Make a religious monthly or seasonal design, such as a Christmas or Easter scene, or use a general design such as a church. Committees of children can easily make the little scenes and change them often

   Note: If you do not care to make a scene, use a seasonal picture

* **Variations** (for a study of musical instruments of the Bible)
   a. Make a 10" harp out of black construction paper and yarn

b. Write titles of new songs on small pieces of construction paper and arrange around harp

c. Rearrange the illustrated design, put song titles on small white harps, and use them as a border

d. Children may also make illustrations of other instruments common in Bible times and add them to the board; this is especially interesting for the older children, but be sure to label them

e. Add pictures of Bible characters such as David playing a harp or Miriam leading the women in dance at the Red Sea

Note: These designs can also be used in poster form. Use felt pens for lettering. Poster chalk also works on construction paper, but use a fixative for permanence.

D. The Sacraments

1. **Baptism:** "Jesus Loves Children"

2. **Source:** Mark 10:13-15

3. **Special emphasis:** Jesus loves all children and wants them to come to Him

4. **Aim or purpose:** To remember that Jesus loves children and wants them to be in His kingdom

5. **Materials needed**

   a. Pink, light green, or light purple for the background
   b. Aqua, red, white, or black letters
   c. Small 2" to 4" hearts of white construction paper or corrugated paper (one for each child)

d. Pictures of children in everyday activities and one picture of Jesus with children

e. A small student picture or snapshot of each student

f. A border of corrugated or construction paper the color of the letters or the heart

* **Variations**

a. Make this into a mission theme by using pictures of children of other lands

b. Use little cutouts of children of other lands on the hearts

c. If no student pictures are available, write a child's name on the heart

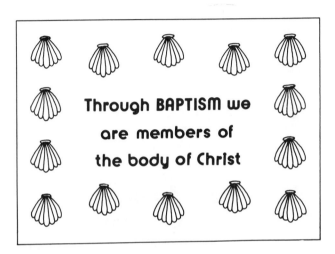

1. **Baptism:** "Through Baptism We Are Members of the Body of Christ"

2. **Source:** Holy Baptism; Eph. 2:19

3. **Special emphasis:** By baptism we become children of God

4. **Aim or purpose:** To establish the truth that we become children of God through baptism

5. **Materials needed**

   a. Aqua burlap for the background

   b. Red or black letters

   c. White construction paper for the shells

   d. Several 4″ or 5″ shell patterns on oak tag or heavy paper

   e. Border if your board is large enough

   Note: Have children trace around shell patterns, cut out, and print their name and date of baptism on their shell. If you wish to save time, ditto shells and have the children cut them out. If some children in the class have not been baptized, let them put their name and birthday on a cross of the same color

* **Variations**

   a. Use blue and green variegated tissue paper for the background, with horizontal lines to simulate water

   b. Let the older children draw their shells freehand, but suggest the size so you have enough room to display all of them

1. **Baptism:** "What Does Baptism Do for You?"

2. **Source:** Holy Baptism; Gal. 3:26-27; Acts 22:16; Mark 16:16; Eph. 2:19

3. **Special emphasis:** The blessings of Baptism

4. **Aim or purpose:** To teach the Scriptural truth that in Baptism our sins are forgiven and we become children of God and receive eternal life.

5. **Materials needed**

   a. Several shades of blue construction paper and shelf paper torn in strips 5″ to 7″ wide and the length of the board to simulate water, with darker shades at the top and bottom
   b. White letters
   c. White construction paper for three shells
   d. Shell pattern about 10″ high
   e. Red, blue, or black felt pens to write phrases on shells

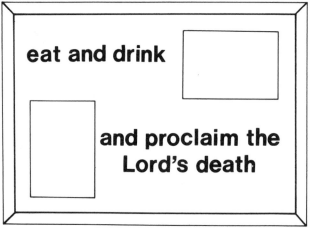

1. **Lord's Supper:** "Eat and Drink"

2. **Source:** Sacrament of the Altar; 1 Cor. 11:26

3. **Special emphasis:** When we partake of the Lord's Supper, we proclaim Jesus' death

4. **Aim or purpose:** To realize that when we eat and drink Christ's body and blood we do show the Lord's death

5. **Materials needed**

   a. Aqua or gold burlap for the background
   b. Red letters for "eat and drink" and "proclaim"
   c. Black letters for the rest of the caption
   d. A 3″ border of black or white construction or corrugated paper
   e. A picture of Jesus on the cross and a picture of the bread and wine, or of communicants receiving the Sacrament
   Note: Church bulletins are a good source for pictures of the Communion elements

* **Variations**

   a. Illustrate the board with symbols of the Lord's Supper or the Crucifixion. For example, use a 10″ to 12″ cross and a chalice with wafer
   b. Try construction paper in gold or brick red for the background, with a corrugated border of white or black

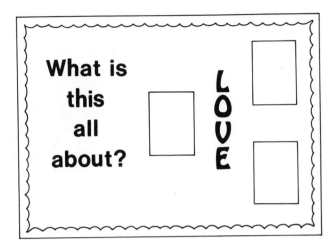

1. **Lord's Supper:** "What Is This All About? Love!"

2. **Source:** Sacrament of the Altar

3. **Special emphasis:** Jesus instituted the Lord's Supper so we could remember His death

4. **Aim or purpose:** To remind us that Jesus instituted the Lord's Supper so we could remember His death by receiving His body and blood

5. **Materials needed**
   a. Light lavender background
   b. Red border
   c. Red letters for the words "this" and "LOVE"
   d. Dark purple or black letters for the rest of the caption
   e. One picture of the Crucifixion for the center, one of Jesus instituting the Lord's Supper, and one of a Communion service, either first Communion or a regular celebration. Mount the three pictures on yellow or white

Pattern Books

Colina, Tessa. *Pattern Book.* Elgin, Ill.: David C. Cook Publishing Co., 1963.

Gilleo, Alma. *Projects and Patterns for Teachers of Young Children.* Elgin, Ill.: David C. Cook Publishing Co., 1965.

Make-It-Yourself Pattern Encyclopedia, comp. Eleanor L. Doan. Glendale, Calif.: Gospel Light Publications, 1962.

Projects and Patterns for Kindergarten Leaders. Elgin, Ill.: David C. Cook Publishing Co., 1967.

Projects and Patterns for Nursery Leaders. Elgin, Ill.: David C. Cook Publishing Co., 1967.

Pattern and Activity Books

Dahl, Anna M. *Handwork Patterns for the Whole Year.* Patterns by Ruth Pistor. Cincinnati: Standard Publishing Co.

Grogg, Evelyn Leavitt. *Kindergarten Pattern Book.* Cincinnati: Standard Publishing Co.

Vonk, Idalee Wolf. *Elementary Activity Patterns.* Cincinnati: Standard Publishing Co.

-----. *Patterns for 52 Visual Lessons: Juniors.* Cincinnati: Standard Publishing Co.

Wonson, Agnes. *Year 'Round Creative Activity Pattern Book.* Cincinnati: Standard Publishing Co.

A Year of Activity Patterns: Primary. Cincinnati: Standard Publishing Co.

Year 'Round Handwork Pattern Book. Cincinnati: Standard Publishing Co.

Year 'Round Patterns. Cincinnati: Standard Publishing Co.

Craft Projects and Activity Books

Adcock, Mabel, and Elsie Blackwell. *Creative Activities.* Anderson, Ind.: Warner Press Co., 1962.

Creative Craft Ideas for All Occasions, ed. Shirley Beegle. Cincinnati: Standard Publishing Co., 1969.

Handcraft Encyclopedia, comp. Eleanor L. Doan. Glendale, Calif.: Sunday School House (Gospel Light), 1967.

301 Creative Crafts for All Occasions, ed. Shirley Beegle. Cincinnati: Standard Publishing Co., 1969.

Teaching Aids Books

Ellingboe, Betty. *Teaching Idea Kit.* Minneapolis: Augsburg Publishing House, 1963.

Make-It-Yourself Visual Aid Encyclopedia, comp. Eleanor L. Doan. Glendale, Calif.: Gospel Light Publications, 1967.

Stencil Pattern Packets

Bible Stencils. Norwalk, Conn.: C. R. Gibson Co. Contemporary and Biblical subjects for Sunday school, vacation Bible school, and home use.

Pre-School Bible Stencils. Norwalk, Conn.: C. R. Gibson Co. Large, simple cutouts of Biblical and contemporary subjects.

The Story of Jesus Stencils. Norwalk, Conn.: C. R. Gibson Co. A set of 36 stencil symbols for illustration, education, and decoration.

Holiday Stencils Art Book. Elgin, Ill.: David C. Cook Publishing Co. Designs for Easter, Christmas, New Year's, etc.

Religious Coloring Books

ABC Bible Coloring Book
ABC Easy to Color Pictures
Be Near Me, Lord Jesus
Bible Pictures to Color
Children Around the World
Color God's Beautiful World
God Cares for Us
God's Children Around the World
God's Children in Many Lands
Helping Jesus
I Have Friends
I'm So Glad
In God's House
Jesus Talks to Me
Little Marcy and Her Friends
My Church
My Friendly Church
Pre-School Bible Pictures to Color
Pre-School New Testament Pictures
See and Hear
Thank You, God, Dot to Dot
Tiny Tots